OH, LOOK! TIS A POEM BOOK!

Davinia Ridgwell

BookLeaf
Publishing

India | USA | UK

Oh, look! Tis a Poem Book!

© 2021 Davinia Ridgwell

Presentation by *BookLeaf* Publishing

Web: www.bookleafpub.com

E-mail: info@bookleafpub.com

ISBN: 9789358361315

First edition 2021

To everyone who believed in me

ACKNOWLEDGEMENT

To Devon, my wonderful lecturer who gave me a chance.

1. THERE'S A DRAGON IN MY GARDEN

There's a dragon in my garden,

Sitting on a leaf.

Curled up in a ball,

And fire he doth breathe.

There's a dragon in my garden,

Claws as sharp as thorns,

And I swear that if I listen,

I can hear a tiny snore.

With a golden body,

And dusty brown wings.

Hazelnut eyes,

This dragon's got everything!

All of a sudden,

His wings spread wide.

And up the dragon flew,

Way out of sight.

There was a dragon in my garden,

But now he has gone away.

However, I still sit near the window,

And I pray.

That one day he will come back,

My newly found friend.

One day he'll visit,

The dragon will visit once again.

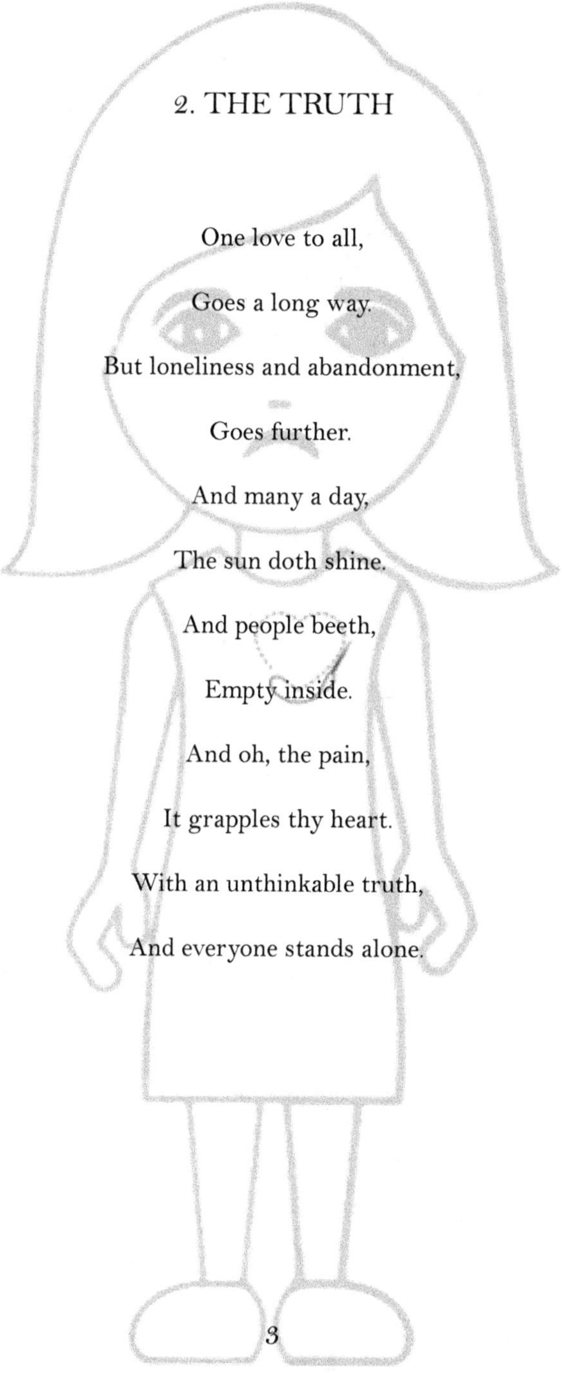

2. THE TRUTH

One love to all,

Goes a long way.

But loneliness and abandonment,

Goes further.

And many a day,

The sun doth shine.

And people beeth,

Empty inside.

And oh, the pain,

It grapples thy heart.

With an unthinkable truth,

And everyone stands alone.

3. THE MEANING OF LIFE IS...

A mother's first child,

a husband's first wife.

A child's first school day,

a teenager's first strife.

A nerd's first payback,

a bully's first smack in the gob.

A student's first pass,

a grownup's first real job.

A couple's first kiss,

in holy matrimony,

What is the meaning of life?

Whatever you want it to be!!

4. THE MEANING OF DEATH IS...

A loved one's passing,

a best friend's end.

A close family relative,

struggling to mend.

The hole left by,

the one who is gone.

But no matter how hard it is,

we must remain strong.

There are people that need love,

And need to be hugged and kissed.

But to those who are above,

You are going to be sorely missed!

5. A WARM SUMMER'S DAY

The moon shines against an endless sea of stars,

And with one almighty gasp blows away the clouds.

The sun sparkles against a rosy quilt of sky,

Warming us once again.

6. IT ALL MAKES SENSE

Hoojamaflip, thingamabob, and a squid-dilly-doo.

Whatchamajig, oogleemabip and a hippiti hoppiti woo.

Squacknify, shocknifant and my valinuntipoo.

They sense no makes.

And yet if the above words are used,

In certain context and ways.

They can be fully understood,

But the nonsense aspect, still stays.

These words always find their way into,

Our everyday vocabulary.

And many people that know me?

Know that my dialect is far from ordinary.

So, I search for a hoojamaflip,

Or a whatchamajig or a squid-dilly-doo.

To squacknify our language,

And to help others to–

Learn how to be shocknifant,

And call their special someone a valinuntipoo.

I reckon it's easy with the help of a thingamabob,

An oogleemabip and a sprinkling of a hippiti hoppiti woo!

7. PEBBLE

9

"Kick the pebble" said John, "Go on, don't be shy". But I didn't want to. I wasn't sure why. I tried to reason with him and come up with multiple excuses. In the end? I just said no. John raised his hand and struck me. "How dare you say no. To me? To me. How dare you say no to me". I bit my lip and looked at John. "Strike me all you want" I said, "But I will not kick that pebble. Nor shall I kick any pebble". Then John started to insult me, and my blood started to boil. I felt the burning rage inside me as with my feelings he did toil. And with one, quick kick, my foot touched the pebble and sent it into the air. It flew so majestically; it was a spectacle to behold. It was so beautiful that John began to cry. It soared, for what seemed forever, until it came to an abrupt stop… in a passing toddler's eye.

8. ONLY FOUR LETTERS

Such a strong, powerful word

and only four letters,

Obey.

Obey Father, Obey Mother,

Obey Sister, Obey Brother.

Obey touch, Obey sound,

Obey straight, Obey around.

Obey college, Obey school,

Obey some, Obey all.

Obey left, Obey right,

Obey black, Obey white.

Obey this, Obey that,

Obey tit, Obey tat.

Obey fast, Obey slow,

Obey stop, Obey go.

Obey pencil, Obey pen,

Obey little, Obey often.

Obey gun, Obey knife,

Obey husband, Obey wife.

Obey girl, Obey boy,

Obey sadness, Obey joy.

Obey Heaven, Obey Hell,

Obey sight, Obey smell.

Obey up, Obey down,

Obey smile, Obey frown.

Obey street, Obey neighbour,

Obey boss, Obey labour.

Obey enemy, Obey friend,

Obey the beginning, Obey the end.

Such a strong, powerful word

and only four letters,

Obey.

9. PAIN IS EVERYWHERE AND ALL AROUND

So ill, but true, one's mind is said to be.

Frozen in time, but we will always live.

No one knows that you need darkness to see,

everyone's got a form of hate to give.

Whether it be real or cybernetic

the pain one causes, never goes away.

The word, sorry? They might lay it on thick

but their plea is easily led astray.

As soon as you close your eyes, evil strikes.

No matter how hard you try, you can't hide

away. Not in any way. From the likes,

of betrayers and fakers who have lied.

And although, in the end, they get busted.

It makes you wonder, who... can be trusted.

13

10. YOU MAKE ME WET

I love the feeling I get from you.

Especially when you kiss my neck.

Sometimes you can go for hours.

I am not jealous,

when you pleasure other people.

Objects can lengthen the fun.

When you are finished,

you leave a mess on the floor.

-I love the rain.

11. CAT

I prowl. My whiskers, all a-twitching as

I pounce! My claws, dig deep into my

prey.

It squirms. But no escape will come its

way.

For if I let it go, what will I eat?

My fur. It must be cleaned with a lick of

my tongue. It is a long and delicate

process. For it must not be brushed the

wrong

way. Never. It does not hurt but annoys

me. So very much. My teeth? They are

sharp.

So that I can tear flesh, free, from a bone.

Be aware. Do not get on the wrong side

of me. As this will leave me with no

choice

but to? Attack! I could be, oh so sweet

but I rather like striking fear instead.

12. A WASP'S HALLOWEEN

Bees, bees, bees.

Sunshine and shadows.

Their hive hanging in the tree.

Tiny, striped, balls of fluff.

Two of them,

come close to me.

But no fear shall

be felt, because- ow!

Although it's rare,

these two have stung me.

One in the hand,

the other in my neck.

All that can be felt,

is a sense of confuzzlement.

Well, that and the

pain from these pricks.

"Why did you do this,

no harm was done to you?".

The bees turn to face me,

with miniature, evil grins.

They hover up close,

and whisper in my ear.

"We're actually wasps,

Happy Halloween, motherfucker".

13. NO MORE

No more shall the shrubbery bloom for Spring.

Nor shall the squirrels make their homely nests.

No more shall the birds softly tweet and sing,

the forest appears empty and depressed.

With beautiful nature, once we were blessed.

Now there's only blackness, shadows, and gloom.

Once we could sit and view a robin redbreast,

Now, I'm afraid a bleak future does loom.

Soon, all we shall see is nothing… but doom.

No more of nature's wondrous finishes.

It puts me into a rather immense fume,

As all the artistry of the world diminishes.

And so, grand Mother Nature's world did fall,

For man came along and quashed it all.

20

14. DEAR, PYJAMAS, DRESSING GOWN AND SLIPPERS

You are what comforts me now,

I hope I never grow.

For if I do, there will be no choice,

you'll simply have to go.

Without any warning,

he just got up and left.

We were all feeling numb,

and mother was bereft.

Down the line,

we learnt the truth.

And what we found out?

It made me hit the roof.

That whore latched onto you,

she knew you were feeling down.

She used your emotions against you,

and ran you into the ground.

Just as you were coming back,

she announced a, big, surprise.

I'm pregnant and it's yours!

But we know this to be a lie.

All is lost

I refuse to believe that everything is over and

I realize this may be a shock, but I have confidence that life will get better.

'The world has gone to shit'.

They will not change my mind

The world will know

I have my priorities straight because

death is more important than

hope. But this will not be true in my era.

People die every second,

experts tell me,

Nothing can be done.

I do not concede that

life can/will be improved.

In the future,

The death toll shall be even bigger. No longer will it be said that the sun can shine through thick clouds.

It will be evident that

we should just give up.

It is foolish to presume that

happiness is everywhere.

And all of this will come true unless we reverse it.

16. A JOURNEY THROUGH THE PAGES

25

There she was,

Sitting by the window.

Her golden hair a flutter in the wind.

A book clasped within her hands,

She was reading.

Her eyes, scanning each page with grace and beauty,

And anger.

Rage, perhaps?

She paused,

placing the book down delicately- ah, a sip of tea.

Back to it.

The reading was normal for a while,

Until tears began to fall,

Oh no.

Wait, was she laughing?

Another sip of tea.

Many strange emotions.

Back to it.

She changes position, for her legs had begun to cramp,

And reads some more.

A careful turn of the page,

More scanning.

Her eyes focusing on every word and sentence,

Her lips pouting in concentration,

Pause.

Thirsty again.

Back to it.

Hours go by,

And yet she's still reading- might even finish tonight?

Wait.

More rage.

She slams the book shut,

Contemplates throwing it at a wall.

Breathes.

Places the item down on the bed- it isn't finished.

A much-needed sip of tea,

More tears.

Ah, the author had killed her favourite character...

Much loss,

Perhaps a break now?

Oh?

She sighs, picking the book up,

Back to it.

17. MOUSE

I scurry and I hurry,

I tear around the house.

I patter and I scatter,

I'm a little brown mouse.

I rush but, in a hush,

I must not be found.

It's scary, so I'm weary,

When the cat's around.

The claws on my paws,

They make a titter tat.

Some cheese? Yes please!

Drop it on the floor with a splat.

I roam about the home,

With my nose all busy twitching.

It's great! It's like fate!

That I live in the kitchen.

I make not a sound as I run around,

Stealing people's food.

A lesson was taught, when once I was caught,

And out of the house I was shooed.

Even at my best, I am but a pest,

I hear the humans say.

They just moan about me, and they groan about me,

Throughout the night and day.

They should remain calm, for I do them no harm,

If you think about it.

If they gave me a chance and didn't run at first glance,

Into the family I reckon I'd fit.

It may take a while, for them to see I'm not vile,

But I'm willing to take the test.

To be, oh so, adored and no longer ignored?

It is my only true quest.

Yes, unlimited food is great, and so is staying up late,

But love is what I crave,

My life of crime and hiding all the time,

Away I would gladly waive.

But there's no way, even though I pray,

They'd let me be their friend.

So away I must hide and wipe away tears that I've cried.

And thus, my tale comes to an end.

18. THE PEN IS MIGHTIER THAN THE SWORD

Injuries tend to heal,

But words can hurt forever.

They seep into your thoughts, and hide out within your mind,

Awaiting their chance to attack.

Relishing in the fact,

They own you for life.

19. GERBIL

My work is never done.

There's always tunnels to be dug,

Tubes to be chewed,

And sand baths to knock over.

A nibble of some food- a quick drink.

Dig, dig, dig, dig.

I rest now.

Just a small nap, wait-

My cage... it's being opened!

Ah... no nap.

Snugs with my owner.

A little purr.

This is fun!

I shall rest now, this time, upon my owner's shoulder.

20. POETRY POEM

Rhyme here, rhyme there,

Rhyming everywhere.

This one rhymes with stanza six.

This line breaks the pattern.

This verse is simply number five,

Poetry is full of tricks.

The first type that we've got

is called a Villanelle.

And it follows a simple plot.

Warning, they can make you fraught,

if you find rhyming a hell.

To write one, you've got

to keep the rhymes nice and taut.

On certain words, you must dwell

to keep to the much-needed plot.

The next type, that I've written

goes by the name, Pantoum.

Only certain words will fit in.

The poem that can cause you gloom.

Goes by the name, Pantoum.

Make sure, you add it to your crew.

The poem that can cause you gloom.

Is nothing compared to,

Sonnets must be formed of 10 syllables,

and they tend to be made up of quatrains.

With the final two stanzas a couplet,

writing them, causes me sizeable pain.

Up next? A type called a Ballad.

Again, it follows a

certain pattern of syllables.

It is the only way

to create one of these poems.

This stanza? It must rhyme.

Not with me but, my friend below,

it happens every time.

And now? Time for a confession,

I absolutely love poetry!

I love reading it,

I love writing it,

It feels like a part of me.

Leading on from that,

it is time for a performance!

A tiny little rap.

It might be crap,

and instead of wanting to clap,

you may want to slap,

me around the face.

Cause you feel a huge distaste,

if this is the case,

you have my attempt of atonement,

I just got lost in the moment.

Now that I've calmed down,

it's time for a Sestina!

The format is quite simple,

let's see if you notice

it. I have no rhyming scheme,

or syllabic pattern,

I have only one pattern,

make sure you note it down.

No need for a rhyming scheme,

with this type of Sestina.

Well, did you notice?

The format is quite simple.

I am a bit more testing,

as I follow a system of rhyme.

There is no room for resting,

I take up a lot of time.

My name? You'll soon be digesting

it. A Rhyming Sestina is what I'm

called. People say that I'm

a tiny bit too testing

and no one has the time.

They are all too busy resting

after struggling with writing rhymes.

Just look at all this info, you're going to be busy digesting.

Cinquains,

they are up next.

No proposal of rhyme.

Certain syllables are needed,

once more.

And thus, we have come to the end,

Of our poetry lesson, my friend.

Use these techniques well.

When you are creating poetry.

Will you be any good?

Only time will tell.

www.ingramcontent.com/pod-product-compliance
Lightning Source LLC
LaVergne TN
LVHW010916200726
843509LV00013B/1959